AGE 7-9

Dr Bill Gillham
Illustrated by Sascha Lipscomb

At this age children can quickly catch up with reading – it's more difficult later on. This book is designed to focus on the basic skills needed for reading: the different ways of recognising words. In English no 'rule' about letters and sounds is 100% true. But if it works 90 – 95% of the time it's worth using.

How to help your child

- Keep sessions short and regular: learning is better when it is spaced out.
- Make sure your child understands what they have to do.
- Encourage your child to ask for help, but give it by asking questions rather than telling the answer.
- Ask your child to show you what they have done: point out mistakes briefly and **praise what they've got right!**
- Don't treat the tests too formally. They are designed to make your child aware of their progress and give them a sense of achievement.
- Remember: fluent reading comes from practice with books that children find **easy**. Use the nine out of ten rule. Ask them to read you a page; if they get more than one word in ten wrong, it's too hard.

The only home learning programme supported by the NCPTA

Letters and sounds

Every letter makes a sound.

Put a tick under each one that you know.
Practise any you're not sure of.

*Remember – a letter's **sound** isn't the same as its **name**.*

a	b	c	d	e

f	g	h	i	j	k	l

m	n	o	p	q	r	s

t	u	v	w	x	y	z

a e i o u are all VOWELS
(and so is **y** when it comes at the end of a word).
All other letters are called CONSONANTS.

First letter sounds

Every word begins with a sound.

Write down the first letter sounds for these pictures, like this:
Practise any you get wrong.

b

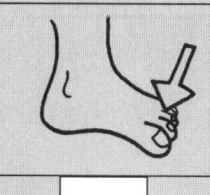    

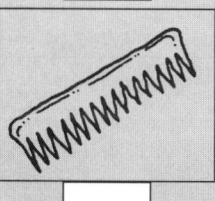 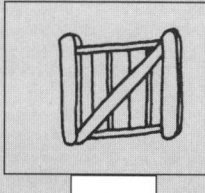 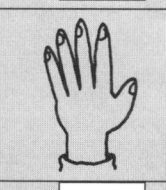  

 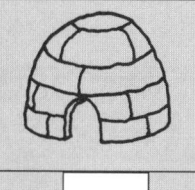 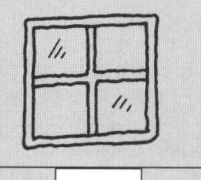 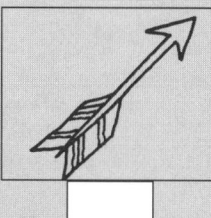 

  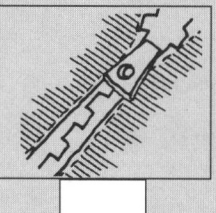  

  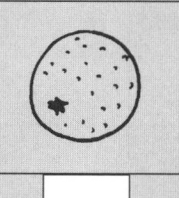  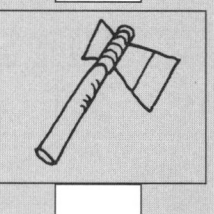

Write down the letter sound in the **middle** of this word.

Special letters

Some letters make two sounds.

a	as in	(a)pple	or	[a]lien
c	as in	(c)up	or	[c]ity
e	as in	(e)gg	or	[e]lastic
g	as in	(g)ap	or	[g]inger
i	as in	(i)nk	or	[i]ron
o	as in	(o)range	or	[o]pen
u	as in	(u)nder	or	[u]niform

And this one makes three.

y   as in   (y)o-yo   or   b[y]   or   sadl⟨y⟩

But only at the **end** of a word!

Match these words by their **first sounds** to the ones in the boxes:

ugly   carpet   enemy   acid
circle   even   gin
on   island   acre   good
invent   unit   only   yellow

Write them here: ▼

apple		orange		ginger	
cup		under		iron	
egg		alien		open	
gap		city		uniform	
ink		elastic		yo-yo	

Which sound?

Read the first two words in this row:

(a)nkle   [a]ngel   a ctor   a corn   a pple   a pe

Now read each of the other words in turn. Put a circle round the first letter if it sounds like the one in the first word:

(a)nkle

and a square round the first letter if it sounds like the one in the second word:

[a]ngel

Now do the same with these:

(c)arrot	[c]inema	c ity	c an	c entre	c amera
(e)mpty	[e]ject	e nd	e lectric	e lbow	e leven
(g)as	[g]iraffe	g ame	g arden	g ents	g eneral
(i)nside	[i]ce	i ron	i t	i ll	i vy
(u)nder	[u]nited	u ncle	u seless	u gly	u nisex
(o)ctopus	[o]ver	o' clock	o tter	o pen	o dd
(y)ellow	st[y]	nearl ⟨y⟩	y es	repl y	fl y	sill y	y esterda y

Put a **diamond** round the third sound y makes.

Special sounds

Some consonants make a different sound when there are two of them together.

Here are the most common ones:

ch	as in	**ch**imney
sh	as in	**sh**op
th	as in	**th**at (hard)
		think (soft)

These make sounds you don't expect:

ph	makes a **f** sound	as in	**ph**one	
ch	makes a **c** sound	as in	**ch**emist	
gh	makes a **g** sound	as in	**gh**ost	
wh	makes a **w** sound	as in	**wh**en	
	or a **h** sound	as in	**wh**o	

There are not many of these.

Mostly you just don't sound the **h** at all.

w̷hat   w̷here   g̷host   c̷hemist

In these words you don't sound the **w**.

w̷hose   w̷ho   w̷hole

Put the right two-letter sounds at the beginnings of the words below.

Choose from: | th | sh | wh | ph | ch |

Like this: | <u>ch</u> ip |

| ___in | ___ank | ___oto | ___ick | ___ampoo |

| ___eat | ___ild | ___elf | ___eep | ___ich |

Now put a circle round the two-letter sounds in these sentences.

For example: (sh)eet

When the sailor fell off his ship, a shark ate him up.

My little brother ate a whole box of chocolates.

A chimney fell off our roof when there was a gale.

I saw three pheasants while I was out walking.

Word endings

Word endings don't always sound as they look.

You don't sound the **e**	**-le**	as in	hand**le**
	-el	as in	parc**el**
	-ed	as in	kick**ed**
You don't sound the **o** ▶	**-our**	as in	col**our**
You don't sound the **a** ▶	**-ar**	as in	calend**ar**

They all say **shun**	**-shion**	as in	cu**shion**
	-sion	as in	televi**sion**
	-tion	as in	sta**tion**

Soft **c**: you don't sound the **e** ▶	**-ce**	as in	dan**ce**
You don't sound the **o** ▶	**-ous**	as in	fam**ous**
You only sound the **t** ▶	**-ght**	as in	ni**ght**
You don't sound it at all ▶	**-gh**	as in	si**gh**
Says **f** ▶	**-gh**	as in	rou**gh**

Am I high enough?

Put the right endings to complete these words.

Choose from here:

ght	tion	gh	ar	el	ous
our	sion	ed	ce	le	shion

ang___ danger___ cu___

arm___ fi___ cou___

hi___ jew___ sta___

begg___ thou___ tremend___

min___ sadd___ peop___

vineg___ tou___ fa___

televi___ turn___ preci___

lo___

Sometimes more than one ending will fit!

brou___

TEST 1

Word beginnings

Choose from these: | th | sh | wh | ph | ch |

1. ____ocolate
2. ____ed
3. ____one
4. ____o
5. ____ey
6. ____imble
7. ____adow
8. ____ite
9. ____eek
10. ____alk

Look at these pictures. What two letters do the words begin with? Write them underneath.

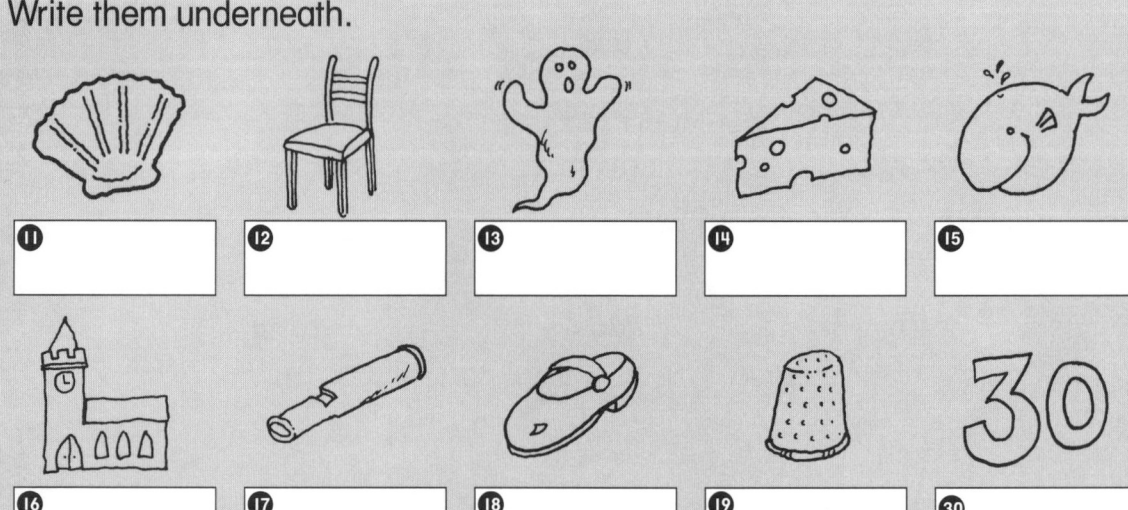

Word endings

Choose from these:

ght	tion	gh	er	ly	ous
ing	sion	ed	ce	ay	shion

21. push____
22. lau____
23. ti____
24. poor____
25. pow____
26. na____
27. fa____
28. str____
29. explo____
30. enorm____
31. pl____
32. prin____

SCORE /32

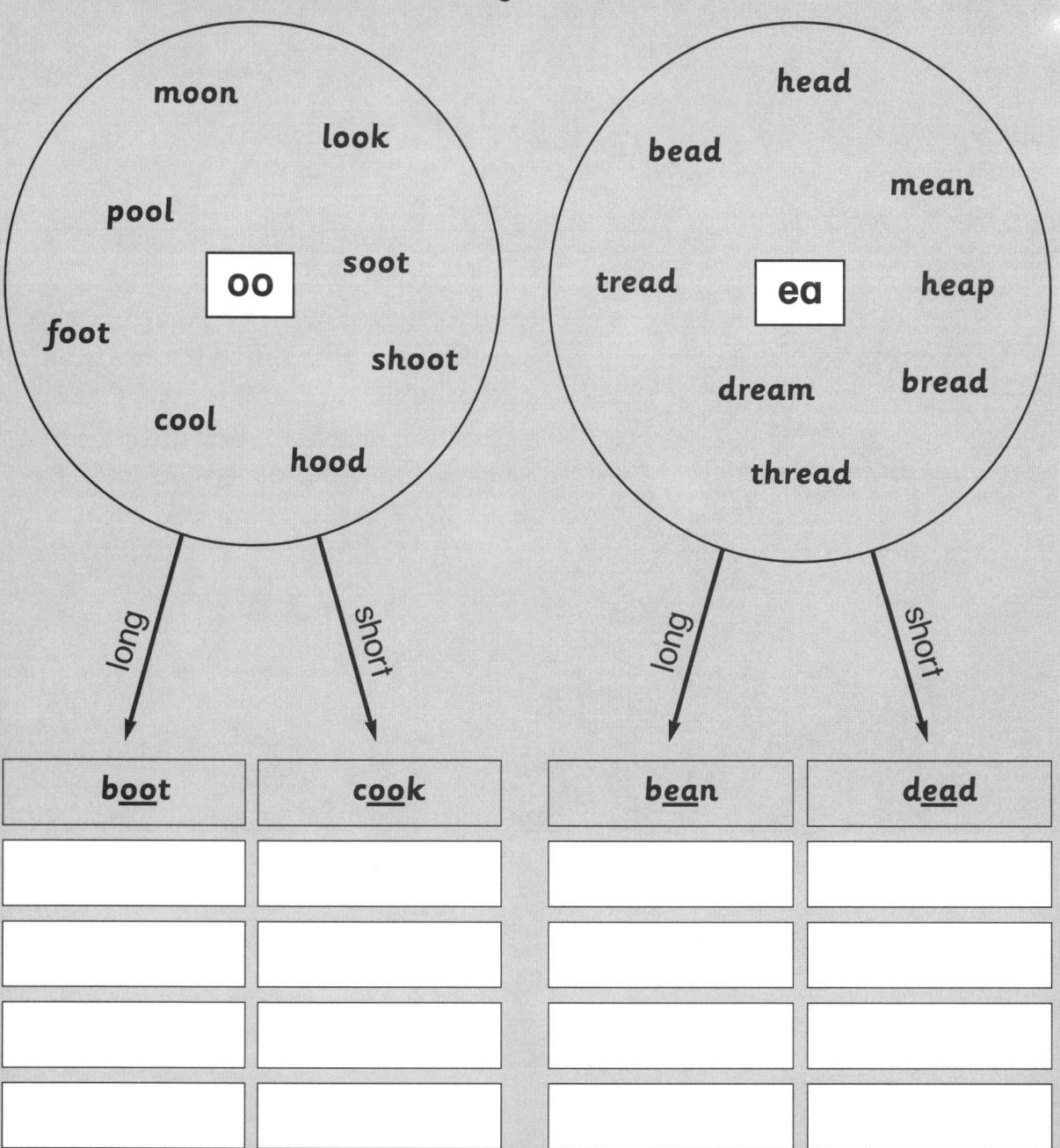

More vowel pairs

For these vowel pairs:

| ay | ai | ee | oa |

you say the name of the first vowel: **a**, **e**, **o**.

But for this pair:

| oi |

you say **oy**.

Can you see these vowel pairs in this story? Put a ring round them.

Gregg checked the nylon chain that joined him to the space station. It was okay. He could stay outside long enough to check the oil inlet. The side of the station was steep, but his load of tools was nothing in zero gravity. He pushed with his heel and floated up. The rays of the sun were bright: he couldn't see very well. No time to waste: the Martian fleet was on its way.

Look at these pictures. Write the vowel pairs for each word underneath.

ee

There is more than one way of saying these vowel pairs.

ie   **ou**   **ow**   ◀ Not a vowel but sounds like one.

ie says the name of the first vowel, **i** ...   **ie**   ... except when it says the name of the second vowel, **e**.

ou says **ow** ...   **ou**   ... except when it comes before **gh** or **ld**.

and **ow** says **ow** ...   **ow**   ... except when it says **oh**.

ou is the one to watch!

Find four more like these:

l<u>ie</u>	ch<u>ie</u>f	l<u>ou</u>d	c<u>ow</u>	l<u>ow</u>

There is more about **ou** on the next page.

ough   ould

There are four ways of saying **ough**.

c**ough**   says   c**off**   Think of another word like it. ▶

th**ough**   says   th**oh**   another like it ▶

en**ough**   says   en**uff**   another like it ▶

th**ough**t   says   th**aw**t   another like it ▶

There are two ways of saying **ould**.

In this one you say the **u** but not the **o**. ▶ c**ould**   b**ould**er ◀ In this one you say the **o** but not the **u**.

Now think of two more of each.

TEST 2

Vowel pairs

ie	ee	oi	oo	oa
ow	ai	ay	ou	ea

Fit the vowel pairs into the gaps in these words.

1. t____gh
2. fl____
3. c____t
4. t____k
5. p____n
6. t____n
7. t____d
8. n____d
9. w____ld
10. m____n
11. f____l
12. p____
13. c____n
14. h____se
15. r____d

Look for the same vowel pairs in this story and put a ring round them.
Score 1 for each vowel pair you find.

The room was grey in the moonlight. The only sound Karen could hear was the beating of her heart. Why had she stayed? Was there really a ghost? She needed to know. She pulled her coat round her and tied the belt. Still no sound. Then a loud bang as the main door burst open, the noise echoing through the rooms.

SCORE / 36

The final 'e' rule

When there's an 'e' at the end of a word, the 'e' has no sound.
But it makes the vowel before it say its name.

not / note

hid / hide

Here are some more examples:

hat → hate
hop → hope

cod → code
fad → fade

See how the final 'e' changes the meaning.

Now add the 'e' to these words and say the new words as you do it.

spin ☐   cap ☐

rob ☐   dam ☐

bit ☐   pan ☐

rat ☐   pip ☐

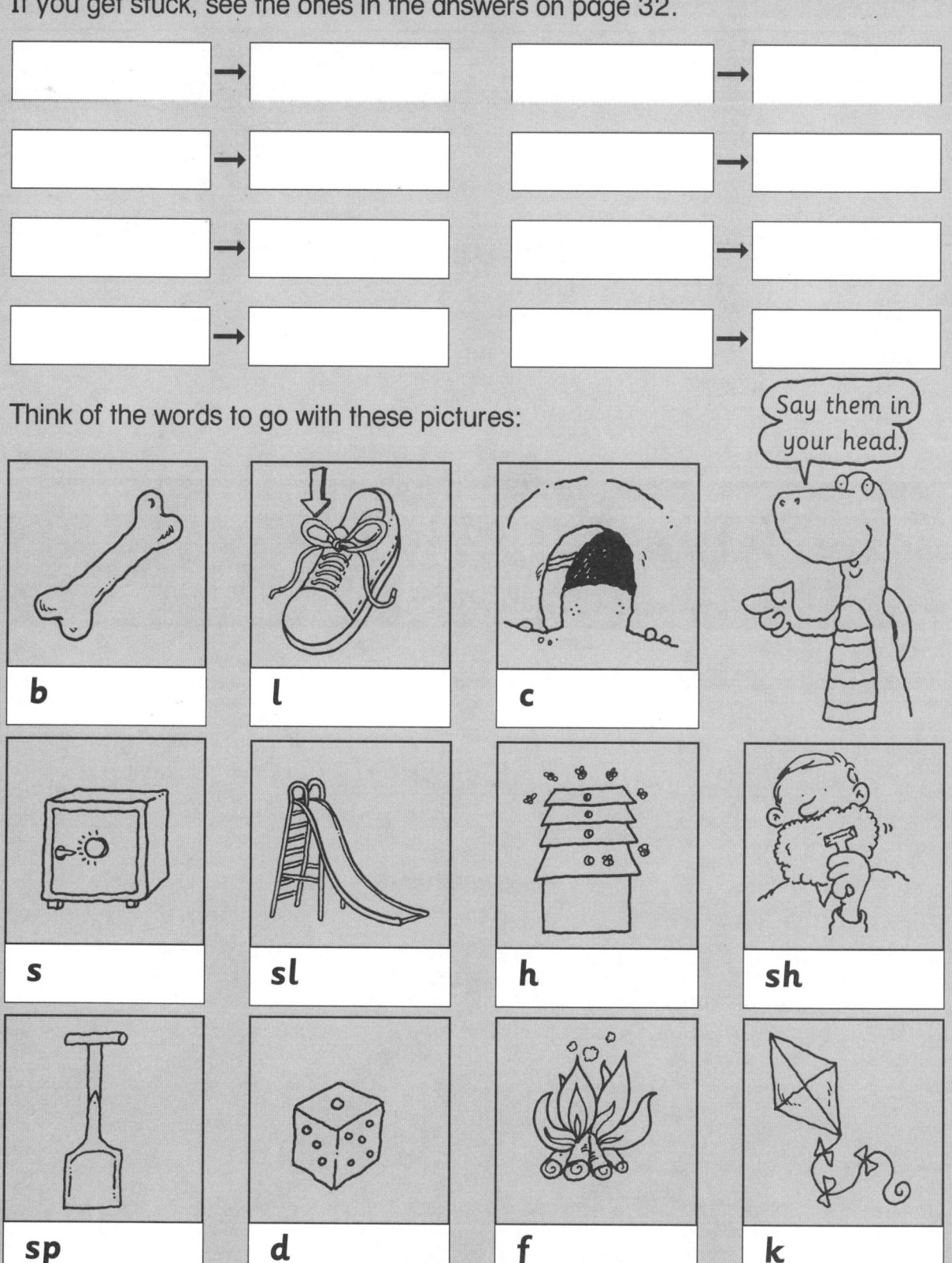

How to read big words

The 'little words' in big words are called **syllables**

Here's a big word broken up into syllables:

pre|his|tor|ic

and another

di|no|saur

Here are the rules.

- A syllable has to sound like a little word but it doesn't have to be a proper word.

   op|po|site

- It has to have at least one vowel in it (a, e, i, o, u, y).

   in|ter|est

- Sometimes a vowel is a syllable on its own.

   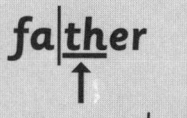
   e|lec|tric

- When there are two consonants together the break usually comes in the middle ...   **pot|ter**

- ... except when they make a sound together.

   fa|ther   **fat|head**
   ↑   ↑↑
   one sound   separate sounds

- Otherwise the break usually comes before the consonant.   **stu|pid**   **cle|ver**

Syllables

Now try these.

Put the syllables in the boxes.

Two syllables

empty

Like this ▶ | emp | ty |

prison

carpet

broken

protect

stupid

appear

inside

dislike

mistake

brother

biscuit

Three syllables

important

Like this ▶ | im | por | tant |

disappear

exciting

separate

parachute

enormous

And now for **four** syllables.

Take your time!
Say the syllables slowly in your head.

intelligent

disappointment

interesting

unimportant

unexpected

ridiculous

electronic

expedition

operation

accidental

That's me!

*That's **not** me!*

Make your own words

So now you can break up words. Let's see if you can put them together!

Make up 10 two-syllable words from these:

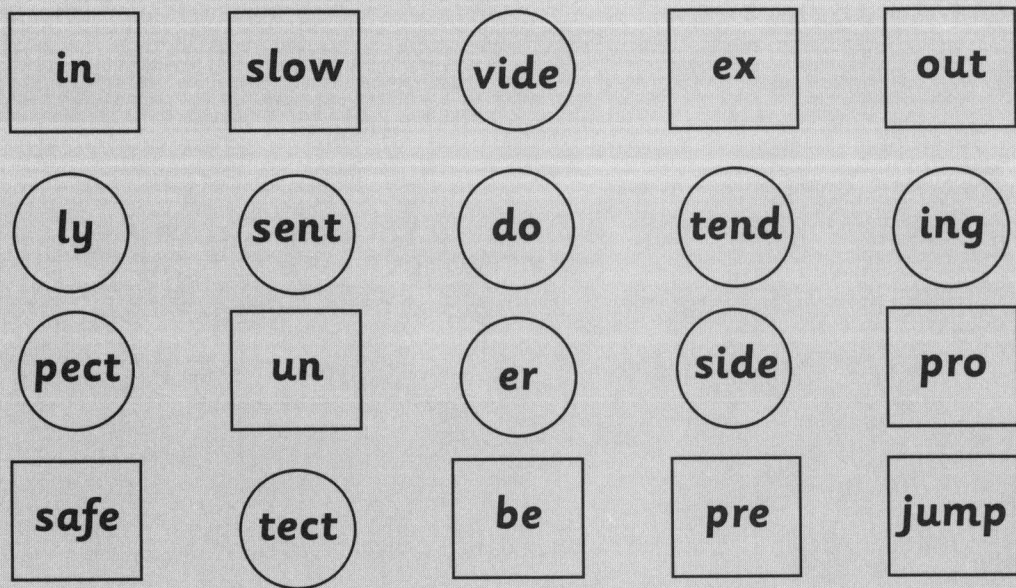

Word beginnings are in ⬚squares⬚.   Word endings are in ◯circles◯.

You can use the same syllable more than once.

1. ☐ ☐   6. ☐ ☐
2. ☐ ☐   7. ☐ ☐
3. ☐ ☐   8. ☐ ☐
4. ☐ ☐   9. ☐ ☐
5. ☐ ☐   10. ☐ ☐

TEST 3

Break up the words by drawing lines down like this:

an|nu|al

The numbers in the squares tell you how many syllables there are.

[2] shower   [3] stepladder   [2] upset   [3] amazing

[4] television   [2] washing   [2] breakfast   [2] pillow

[4] excavation   [3] stereo   [3] presently   [3] underground

Put the syllables in the boxes.

spider □□

butterfly □□□

telephone □□□

computer □□□

operation □□□□

snuggle □□

envelope □□□

formula □□□

particular □□□□

Score 1 for each correct syllable.

SCORE / 60

Which word?

If you don't know a word, the other words in the sentence can help you work out what it is.

Like this:

Our cat caught a little _____.

It could be **mouse** or it could be **bird**.

If you know how the word starts that's a big help.

Like this:

Our cat caught a little r_____.

It could be **rat** or it could be **rabbit**.

None of these is right!

Our cat caught a little ro_____.

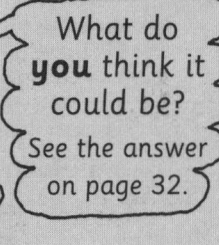

What do **you** think it could be? See the answer on page 32.

Now try these on the next page.

There are three words to choose from in each of the following sentences.
Only one of them is right. Put a ring round the right word.

Like this:

- Because it was raining he put a | cap / cup / can | on his head.

No points for funny answers!

1. Sam had so much to eat that he was | stick / sitting / sick | .

2. When a wheel came off the car it | crashed / crept / carried | into a wall.

3. With a pin she | burnt / burst / bought | all the children's balloons.

4. The crocodile cleaned her | toes / tomatoes / teeth | with a toothbrush.

5. The goalkeeper kicked the | bell / belt / ball | into his own goal.

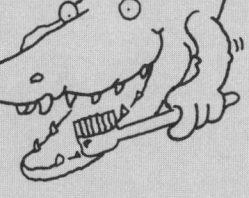

Choose the word

There are ten sentences, each with a word missing.
Choose the right word to go in the gap.

| bit | snake | broke | computer |

| toast | rocket |

| motorbike | birthday | spider | goal |

1. Our dog _____ the postman.

2. I am ten years old on my next _____.

3. I play in _____ for our football team.

4. There was a _____ with long legs in the bath.

5. When I dropped the plate it _____ into pieces.

6. I had _____ and marmalade for breakfast.

7. I like playing games with my _____.

8. My brother rides his _____ to work.

9. The _____ escaped from the zoo.

10. I went to the moon in a _____.

The arrow game

Each word leads to the next word.

Join up the words to make a sentence.
The first one is done for you.

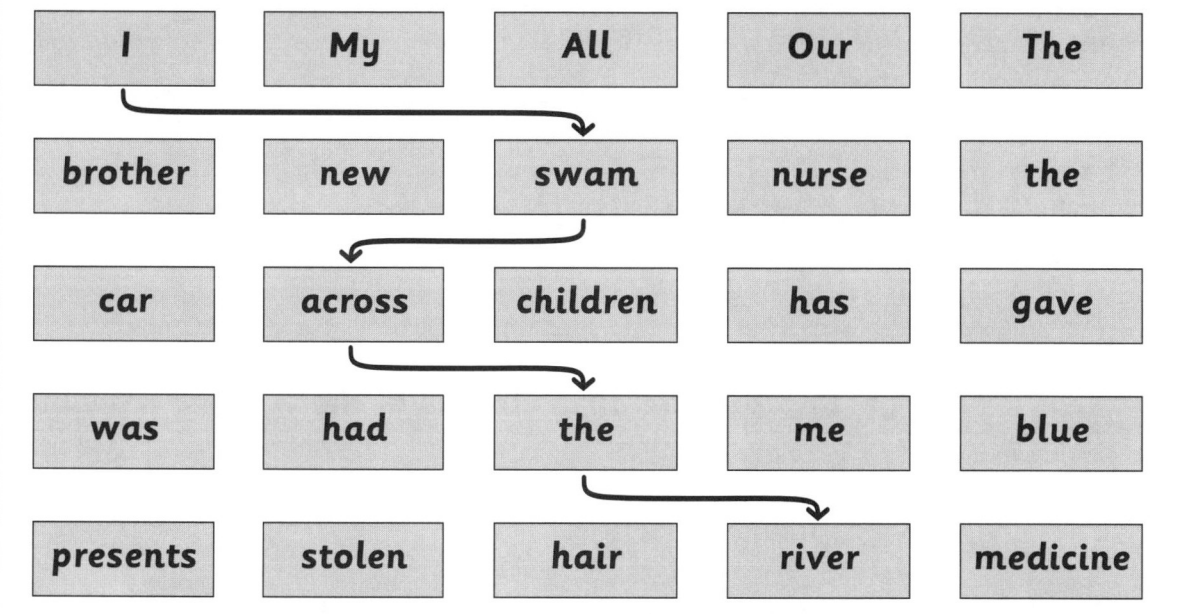

Now do it across.

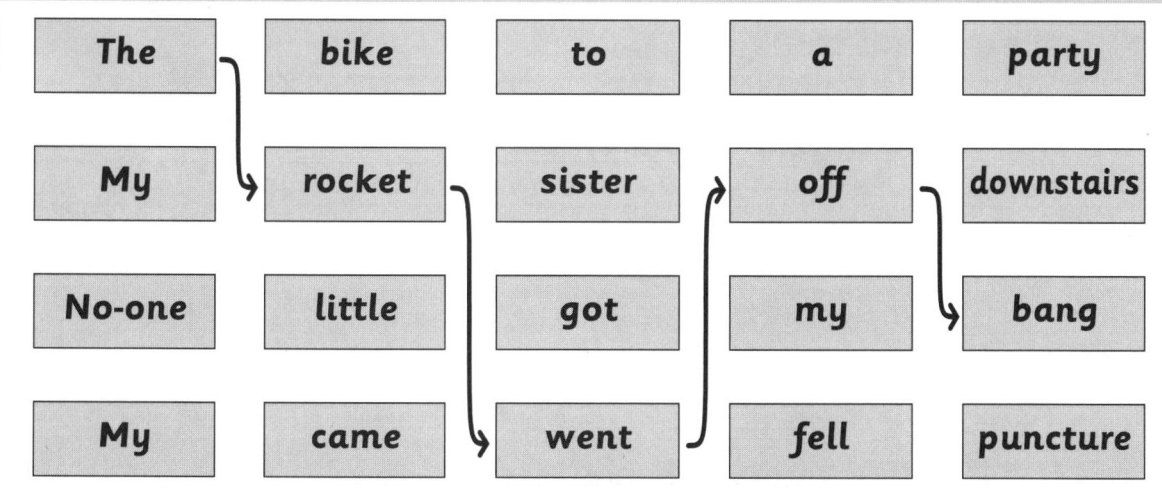

Silly sentences

Silly sentences have the words in the wrong order like this ...

- new likes our nobody teacher.

Nobody likes our new teacher.

▲ You put them in the right order underneath.

... or a word that doesn't make sense, like this:

- **Dad put the dirty clothes in the ~~wishing~~ washing machine.**

▲ You cross out the word that's wrong and put the right word in.

Now correct these 'silly sentences':

1. my lorry mum drives a big.

2. Our cat is afraid of rice.

3. caught house fire door the next.

4. I like hating fish and chips.

5. escaped a circus from the lion has.

6. I had corn flaps for breakfast.

7. my little pool into the brother fell.

8. The sky was full of dark clowns.

9. my tin thumb his opening cut a dad.

10. I dived into the slimming pool.

11. some frightened spiders of people are.

12. We picked all the angles off the tree.

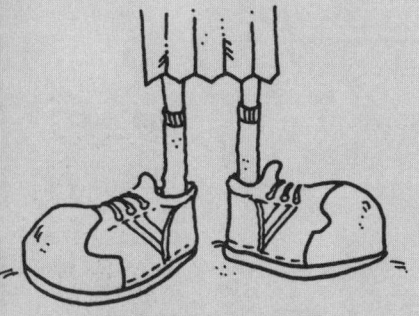

13. my too big are new trainers.

14. When I was ill the donkey came to see me.

Secret letter

Here's a secret letter that has some words missing.
Fill them in to find out the message.

A sub_____ will be opposite the li_____house at midnight on Mon_____ 13th April and again at the same _____ for three days until you signal. Show a light — two sh_____ flashes and one long. The code w_____ is EAGLE. Do not use a car or carry a g_____ Say you are on a camping hol_____ but don't talk too much to anyone. Spies know that y_____ are in the area. Contact me only in an em_____

008

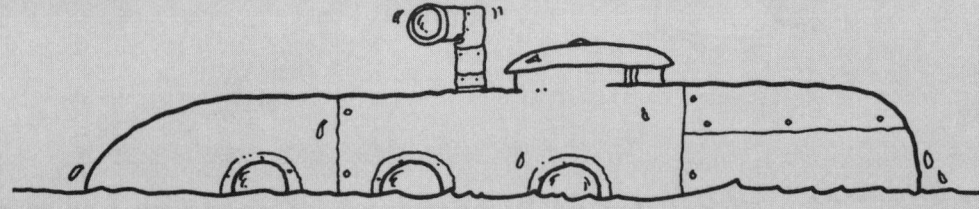

TEST 4

Complete or correct the following sentences:

1. I painted a _____ of our dog.

2. Mum fried some bacon and e_____ .

3. On my birthday Dad [baked / barked / banged] me a cake.

4. _____ Mum put a new tyre on the while.

5. all my face I spots over have.
   _____

6. I blew up the _____ until it burst.

7. Our pet r_____ likes carrots.

8. When the plane had taken off all the passengers had a [mail / meal / moon].

9. _____ My brother fell over and cut his hood.

10. A bee _____ me on the arm.

11. I stuck a stamp on the l_____ .

12. I caught a [fork / fist / fish] with my new rod.

13. _____ I sewed up some wood for the fire.

14. a postman parcel brought the me.
    _____

SCORE /14

Answers

Page 3
t k n u l; c g h r f; s i w
a d; e q z y p; m v o j x

Page 4
acid, carpet, enemy, good, invent,
on, ugly, acre, circle, even,
gin, island, only, unit, yellow

Page 5
(a)ctor, (a)corn, (a)pple, (a)pe;
(c)ity, (c)an, (c)entre, (c)amera,
(e)nd, (e)lectric, (e)lbow, (e)leven;
(g)ame, (g)arden, (g)ents, (g)eneral;
(i)ron, (i)t, (i)ll, (i)vy;
(u)ncle, (u)seless, (u)gly, (u)nisex;
(o)'clock, (o)tter, (o)pen, (o)dd;
(y)es, repl(y), fl(y), sill(y), (y)esterda(y)

Page 7
(top): thin/shin/chin, thank, photo,
chick/thick, shampoo, wheat, child,
shelf, sheep, which
(bottom): (wh)en, (th)e, (sh)ip, (sh)ark;
bro(th)er, (wh)ole, (ch)ocolates;
(ch)imney, (wh)en, (th)ere;
(th)ree, (ph)easants, (wh)ile

Page 9
angle, dangerous, cushion; armour, fight,
cough; high, jewel, station; beggar,
thought, tremendous; mince, saddle,
people; vinegar, tough, fashion;
television, turned, precision; lotion,
brought (but others are possible)

TEST 1 Page 10
(top): chocolate, shed, phone, who, they;
thimble, shadow, white, cheek, chalk
(middle): shell, chair, ghost, cheese,
whale; church, whistle, shoe, thimble, thirty
(bottom): pushing/pushed, laugh, tight,
poorly, power, nation; fashion, string,
explosion, enormous, play, prince
(others possible)

Page 11

Long	Short	Long	Short
moon	foot	mean	head
pool	look	bead	tread
cool	soot	heap	bread
shoot	hood	dream	thread

Page 12
(top): chain, joined, okay, stay, oil, steep,
load, heel, floated, rays, see, fleet, way
(bottom): sheep, boat, rain, paints, tray,
coin, feet, point, coat, spray

Page 13
tie, pie, cried, tried; thief, believe, field,
shield; found, sound, house, shout; how,
town, crown, brown; tow, mow, show,
blow (and others like this)

Page 14
(top): trough, dough, rough, fought
(bottom): should, would, shoulder, mould
(and others like this)

TEST 2 Page 15
(top): tough, flea, coat, took, pain; town,
tied, need, would, mean; fool, pay, coin,
house, read (others possible)
(bottom): room, moonlight, sound, could,
hear, beating, heart, stayed, really,
needed, know, coat, round, tied, sound,
loud, main, door, noise, through, rooms

Page 16
spine, robe, bite, rate; cape, dame,
pane, pipe

Page 17
(top): fin, fine, hug, huge, sit, site, fat,
fate, kit, kite, can, cane, mad, made,
man, mane (and many others)
(bottom): bone, lace, cave; safe, slide,
hive, shave; spade, dice, fire, kite

Page 20
(two): pri son, car pet, bro ken,
pro tect, stu pid, ap pear, in side,
dis like, mis take, bro ther, bis cuit
(three): dis ap pear, ex ci ting,
sep ar ate, par a chute, e nor mous

Page 21
in tel li gent, dis ap point ment,
in ter es ting, un im por tant,
un ex pec ted, ri dic u lous, e lec tron ic,
ex pe di tion, op er a tion, ac ci den tal
(Small differences in your answers are
acceptable.)

Page 22
slowly, provide, expect, intend, undo,
jumping, safely, outside, present, beside,
protect, slower (and others like this)

TEST 3 Page 23
(top): show er, step lad der, up set,
a ma zing, tel e vi sion, wash ing,
break fast, pil low, ex ca va tion,
ste re o, pre sent ly, un der ground
(bottom): spi der, but ter fly,
tel e phone, com pu ter, o per a tion,
snug gle, en ve lope, for mu la,
par tic u lar

Page 24
robin

Page 25
1 sick, 2 crashed, 3 burst, 4 teeth, 5 ball

Page 26
1 bit, 2 birthday, 3 goal, 4 spider,
5 broke, 6 toast, 7 computer,
8 motorbike, 9 snake, 10 rocket

Page 27
(top): My brother has blue hair.
All the children had presents.
Our new car was stolen.
The nurse gave me medicine.
(bottom): My bike got a puncture.
No-one came to my party.
My little sister fell downstairs.

Page 28
1 My mum drives a big lorry.
2 Our cat is afraid of mice.
3 The house next door caught fire.
4 I like eating fish and chips.

Page 29
5 A lion has escaped from the circus.
6 I had corn flakes for breakfast.
7 My little brother fell into the pool.
8 The sky was full of dark clouds.
9 My dad cut his thumb opening a tin.
10 I dived into the swimming pool.
11 Some people are frightened of
   spiders.
12 We picked all the apples off the tree.
13 My new trainers are too big.
14 When I was ill the doctor came to see
   me.

Page 30
submarine, lighthouse, Monday, time,
three, short, word, gun, holiday, you,
emergency

TEST 4 Page 31
1 picture, 2 eggs, 3 baked, 4 wheel,
5 I have spots all over my face,
6 balloon, 7 rabbit, 8 meal, 9 head,
10 stung, 11 letter, 12 fish, 13 sawed,
14 The postman brought me a parcel.

ISBN 0 340 67270 6
Text copyright © 1996 Bill Gillham
Illustrations copyright © 1996 Sascha Lipscomb

The rights of Bill Gillham to be identified
as the author of this work has been asserted by him in
accordance with the Copyright, Design and Patent Act 1988.

First published in Great Britain 1996. Printed and bound in Great Britain.

10 9 8 7 6 5

All rights reserved. No part of this publication may be reproduced,
stored in a retrieval system, or transmitted, in any form or by any
means, without the prior written permission of the publisher, nor be
otherwise circulated in any form of binding or cover other than that
in which it is published and without a similar condition being
imposed on the subsequent purchaser.

Published by Hodder Children's Books, a division of Hodder
Headline plc, 338 Euston Road, London NW1 3BH.

A CIP record is registered by and held at the British Library.